# The Happily Ever After?

Catina Noble

crowecreations.ca

The Happily Ever After? © 2022 Catina Noble
First Crowe Creations Print Publication May 2022

Front cover photo needpix.com sully-579644_1280
Cover Design © 2022 Crowe Creations
Interior design by Crowe Creations
Text set in Arial; headings in Andalus

Crowe Creations ISBN: 978-1-927058-91-6

To whom it may impact.

# Foreword

Once again, Catina Noble has produced a piece of work that makes us not only think, but feel and wonder and thank the Fates.

I, too, was with my mother when she passed. I, too, had issues with my mother. Having issues with a wounding mother does nothing to lessen the pain of losing her. Believe me. It can make the pain worse.

Sherrill Wark,
author of the poetry chapbook,
*The Closet Hides a Flight of Stairs*

# The Wolf and
the House of Straw

# Take a Breath and...

No improvement but I must…

How are you feeling today, Mom?

I'm only in pain on days that end in y.
Feet shuffle toward the well-used bed.

I pick up her frail right hand and
envelope my left around hers.

She closes her eyes and inhales deeply.

I close mine and hold my breath and
will the tears to stay fast because
now we know
        the cancer is back
            and that means

no transplant
        and a lot of other noes.

No improvement but I must…

How are you feeling today, Mom?

I'm only in pain on days that end in y.

# Over the River and through the Woods to Grandmother's House I Go

# Visits with Gram

No matter how old I got I never got tired of
sitting beside you as close as I could get on
the couch because I could truly feel the love
emanating from you. I always touched both
your hands to make sure I wasn't playing favorites.
I would run my pointy finger across each of your

glossy nails and tell you how pretty they were.
My eyes would always linger over
the hundreds of photos of kids
beautifully framed. They hung on the walls, sat
on the table. They were everywhere and
even though I knew every place my face

presented itself, I pretended I didn't.
Sometimes we would have sleepovers
and I liked those best because in the morning
you would make me toast with real butter
sprinkled with sugar and
the tastiest cup of tea.

# Rings of Magic

I admired all the beautiful gold rings
       that kissed all your fingers,
some more than others.

Their stories were familiar to me
       but I always needed to hear them
just one more time.

Where did you get this ring from,
       who gave it to you and why.
Sometimes you would slip off

the precious kisses and slide them
       onto my tiny fingers and
let me hold them briefly as I gently

fingered the diamonds. I imagined myself
       as a beautiful princess who could remain in
this impenetrable fairy-tale castle.

# No Magic Potions, though...

At school the other kids
would talk about
baking cookies with
their grandma.

The thought of that
was completely
foreign to me so
I always bragged that mine
watched cool television shows.

Of course the kids were always
skeptical, believing the shows
would be boring until
I mentioned how we
loved to watch wrestling and
whoop and holler.

My classmates' jaws would drop
in envy. I would smile with
satisfaction.

# A Granted Wish

Walking into your bedroom always felt like a privilege.
Along your vanity, more colors of nail polish stood
proudly, always facing in the same direction,
all the colors of the rainbow
and more.

My eyes would light up as I wondered what
each color would look like on my own
fingernails and sometimes you
would let me pick one to take home
and gently place

it in my pocket so my parents wouldn't see,
then hold your finger to your lips
to remind me it was our
little secret.

# The Wolf and
# the House of Sticks

# As the Well Runs Dry

Dialysis, cancer and yet that is not enough.
Even she didn't know until she came down with
a cold complete with a coughing fit
that left her in so much pain she rode an
ambulance to the hospital to find out what
body part she must have lost during the process.
All body parts seemed accounted for
yet the pain continued and so did the testing.
Blood, x-rays and medications are checked.
Heart monitor says all is fine and yet she still
curls up and cries but I am not allowed to.
I am supposed to be the strong daughter.
But it is so very hard.
I tell her I need to go to the bathroom
to have few minutes to myself and let at least
a few of these tears out before I break down and let
all of them flow at once and that would not be
okay because it would scare her and it
would scare me. A chance that I would drown.
And isn't this enough for now?
So the hours tick by and all we can do is wait.

# Instructions

Step 1    Inhale deeply. Exhale deeply.

Step 2    Smile, no matter what.

Step 3    Walk through the hospital doors.

Step 4    Find the silver lining even though your heart feels as though it's being crushed.

Step 5    Remind yourself every thirty seconds on a loop that it's about Mom and not you.

Step 6    Don't mention anything that might stress her out.

Step 7    Make sure you have at least one tad, one bit of news, or she will know.

Step 8    Act like everything is fine.

Step 9    Save those tears for later.

Step 10    Exhale deeply. Inhale deeply.

# Escalator Adventures

I remember giggling as we approached
hand-in-hand toward
the escalator in the mall.
For me it was a game but
for you it was a true fear of heights.

Together we would stand at the bottom waiting and
letting other people get on
the escalator and you
changing your mind.

We are going up, we are.
Not going up, we aren't.

We step forward and
your hand releases mine.
I am slowly but steadily moving up
the escalator as you
remain at the bottom worried
until I'm back in your arms after
my name is called over the intercom and
an employee accompanies me to
where you still stand.

# Dessert

You always had a sweet tooth,
letting me know what kind of pie
or cake

you ate for breakfast.
I wondered if your choices would
change but they never did.

Black Forest cake,
blueberry or apple pie so
still every time

I walk by a bakery I
check to see if they have
Black Forest cake

because that was your
favorite and it
reminds me of you.

# Hands

The highlight of her day was
seeing her eyes light up
as she entered her room.
Moments later she would inch
closer to the hospital bed.

Oftentimes her fingers would
slowly make their way over to
her left hand, her smile would deepen
as their hands lay clasped together.

A sigh of relief is gently released from
mother and daughter.

# Holding On

She lies there on the bed.
        Periodically her body
shudders and I wonder
        if it's because of what she's
thinking or if it's from the cold.

No matter the temperature outside or
        in her room or how many
blankets or quilts cuddle her,
        the cold
refuses to part.

# Just One Question?

She tells me
my being by her side is enough.
I feel like it isn't.
I want to offer something
but
months go by and I continue to wonder.
I don't know anything about her even though
she is my mother.

I hold back tears as it occurs to me that
after she is gone
I will no longer be able to ask
questions that
this means I must ask
as many as I can now.

So I ask the biggest and what I believe to be
the most important question first.

Mom, what are your regrets because
I want to make sure I learn from you.

She smiles. Clears her throat.
Too many.

She closes her eyes and squeezes my hand.

The Wolf and
the House of Bricks

# Cobwebs

Over the years, cobwebs
emerged in her house,
in her voice,
in her hair,
in her clothes and
in her mind.

All this in the name of
heartache,
his demands,
nasty words and
items tossed on a whim.

We bore witness.

It's time to clean the cobwebs
from our house,
from our voice,
from our hair,
from our clothes and
from our minds.

We will make different choices and
the poison will slowly fade away as
we take our cobwebs down
one strand at a time.

We bore witness.

# Acknowledgments

Special thanks go to my BFF, my mother of another daughter, Sherrill Wark (Crowe Creations), who pushed me into writing this.

She convinced me she needed—was "itching"—to finally learn the ins and outs of her "new" Affinity Publisher program and wanted a Guinea pig to practice on for free.

I believed her but I sometimes think she has ulterior motives, motives that could make her either the wicked witch or the fairy godmother. Some days, I have trouble deciding which and this makes her laugh and tell me she loves me no matter what I think of her.

# About the Author

Catina Noble is an Ottawa writer with over two hundred publications including books, articles, short stories and poetry. Her work has appeared in many publications including *Woman's World Magazine*, *Chicken Soup for the Soul*, *Bywords*, *Riverview Park Review*, *PEN*, *YTravel Blog*, *The Mindful Word*, *Mojito Mother*, and *Baby Post*. Her poem "You Can't See Me" took first place in the Canadian Authors Association's National Capital Writing Contest in 2014. Three of her books have received the Reader's Favorite Five Star award: *Vacancy at the Food Court & Other Short Stories*; *I'm Glad I Didn't Kill Myself*; and *Everest Base Camp: Close Call*. In 2006, Catina graduated from Algonquin College with her Social Services Worker Diploma and in 2009, she graduated from Carleton University with a Bachelor's Degree in Psychology. She works full time in her field, writes, and is currently enrolled in the Addictions & Mental Health Program at Algonquin College.

# Books by Catina Noble

*El Camino on a Wrecked Ankle* (non-fiction)
*Everest Base Camp: Close Call* (non-fiction)
*Vacancy at the Food Court & Other Short Stories* (fiction)
*Not Just Me* (fiction, Part 1 of the Teal Trilogy)
*Not Again* (fiction, Part 2 of the Teal Trilogy)
*This is It* (fiction, Part 3 of the Teal Trilogy)
*Lost at 13* (non-fiction)
*I'm Glad I Didn't Kill Myself* (non-fiction)
*Katzenjammer* (poetry)
*Finding Evie* (fiction)

Available in print or digital from the Amazon dots.